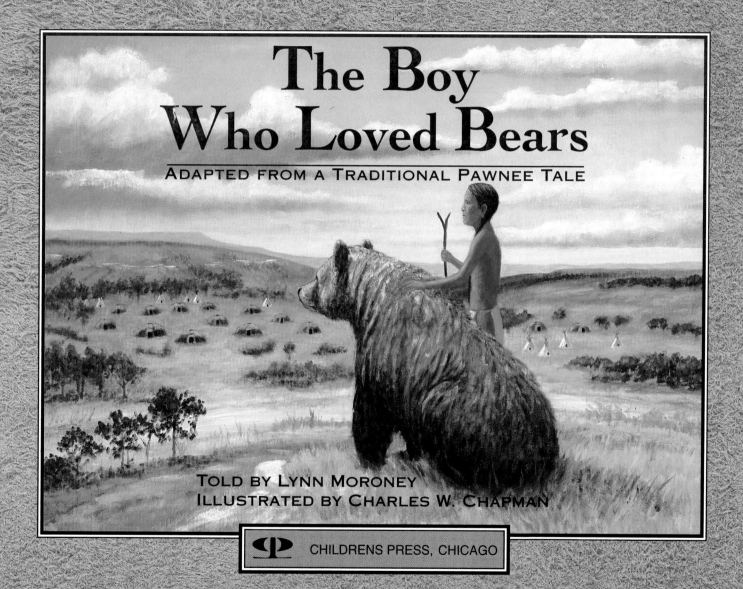

The Boy
Who Loved Bears

ADAPTED FROM A TRADITIONAL PAWNEE TALE

TOLD BY LYNN MORONEY
ILLUSTRATED BY CHARLES W. CHAPMAN

CHILDRENS PRESS, CHICAGO

For Francis — L.M.

I would like to dedicate this book to the preservation of the grizzly bear, an animal close to extinction because of the loss of its habitat. It is my hope that all species will be preserved for the children of many tomorrows. — C.W.C.

Library of Congress Cataloging-in-Publication Data

Moroney, Lynn.
   The boy who loved bears / told by Lynn Moroney : illustrated by Charles W. Chapman.
      p.   cm. — (Adventures in storytelling)
      Summary: In this traditional Pawnee legend, a young hunter learns the secret powers of the bear.
   ISBN 0-516-05142-3
   1. Pawnee Indians — Folklore. 2. Pawnee Indians — Religion — Juvenile literature. 3. Bears — Folklore. [1. Pawnee Indians — Folklore. 2. Indians of North America — Folklore. 3. Folklore — North America. Bears — Folklore.]
I. Chapman, Charles W., ill. II. Title. III. Series.
E99.P3M67   1994   94-9067
398.2'089975 — dc20   CIP
[E]   AC

Introduction

Many versions exist of the following story, which has been told by Pawnee people for centuries. The tale is thought to have originated from a Pawnee Bear Doctor's life story about how he received the healing power of the bear, learned the secrets of the bear ceremony, and passed on the power to others. Oral and written accounts of this story will vary. Although most are found within the oral traditions of the Pawnee people, some have been written down and can be found in folktale collections such as *Pawnee Hero Stories and Folktales* by George Bird Grinnell.

The following adaptation of the story focuses on the spiritual bond between a young Pawnee boy and a bear. The boy's father has saved the life of a bear cub. Eventually, the favor is returned. Thereafter, the boy possesses the healing power of the bear and shares a spiritual bond that continues for generations.

The setting for this story is an area of the western Plains in the United States, now known as the state of Nebraska, where Pawnee people once lived. Pawnee history dates back more than 700 years and is suspected to go far into antiquity. By 1857, as a result of unfair treaties with the United States government, the Pawnee had lost most of their land. Like so many other Native Americans at this time, the Pawnee were forced to leave their homeland and move to territory in the present state of Oklahoma. Today, Pawnee live all over the world, although most live in or around Pawnee, Oklahoma, which is where their Council House is located.

There are today, as in the past, four bands in the tribe — the Skiri (also spelled Skedee), the Chaui, the Pitahawirata, and the Kitkahahki. Each band has two chiefs who sit on the Nasharo (Chiefs) Council. From this council, one head chief is selected. The other tribal governing body is the Pawnee Indian Business Council, which is selected by tribal election.

Long ago, a Pawnee man was returning to his village after a long day of hunting. He was passing by the place where bears were often seen, when he found a baby bear. Cold and hungry, the little bear was crying for his mother. The hunter took pity on the cub and stopped to help him.

After being fed, the cub fell asleep in the hunter's arms. As the hunter looked down at the cub, he thought, "My wife is with child now. Soon I shall hold my own child as I hold this little bear. I pray that if someday my child is in need, someone will offer help."

The hunter made a small medicine bag, filled it with tobacco, and tied it around the bear's neck. He laid the sleeping cub on the ground and covered him with leaves. "Sleep well little one," he whispered. "Your mother will return soon."

When the hunter reached his village, he told his wife about finding the bear and protecting him with the medicine bag. His wife said, "I saw a bear today as well, but I did not look into his eyes."

7

A few days later, the hunter's wife gave birth to a baby boy. The baby was named Little Bear because his parents had seen bears right before his birth.

Many winters passed. Little Bear had grown into a fine hunter. In many ways he seemed to be much like a bear. With his keen sense of smell, he could track animals and hunt, just like a bear.

9

Just like a bear, he was swift in catching fish in streams and rivers, and he always knew where to find the juiciest berries.

10

Often, Little Bear went to the special place of the bears. He brought them gifts, sang songs, and prayed for their protection. There he could feel their power. Sometimes he felt that he was a bear!

11

Young Pawnee boys saw all that Little Bear did. They admired his skills and tried to match his courage when they were hunting. They began calling him "the boy who loves bears."

One day, several young Pawnee were out hunting when they heard the shouts of their enemies. Outnumbered and surrounded, the hunters were unable to defend themselves. After a terrible battle, the enemy rode away, but not until they had killed all the young Pawnee hunters, including the boy who loved bears.

Now all of this happened in the place of the bears, so it was not long before a husband and wife bear came along. Seeing the bodies of the young men, they began to go from one to another.

Soon the wife bear cried out, "Husband, look! It is the boy who prays for us and leaves us food. Can you help him?" "I cannot," he answered. "My medicine works only in the sun, and this day is covered with clouds." But just at that moment the clouds parted, and the sun shone upon the body of Little Bear.

15

And so it was, that for the rest of the day the sun came and went. Each time the sun appeared, the bear used his power to help the boy. "Return life to this youth," he prayed. Slowly, the young hunter's body became warm. Soon he could breathe. Then he could move. In time, Little Bear returned to life.

When Little Bear heard the bear speaking to him, he sat up. "Your wounds are very deep," said the bear. "You cannot make the journey back to your village until you are completely healed. Come live with us until you are well."

The bears guided Little Bear to their cave. For many days and nights he stayed with them. They tended his wounds and taught him all the ways of the bears.

Weeks later, after Little
Bear had fully recovered,
he and the bear began the
long journey back to the
Pawnee camp.

When they reached a ridge overlooking the encampment, the bear said, "Your mother and father have been worrying. Go first to them and let them know you are alive and well. Then return to me."

20

Little Bear did as he was told. Upon entering the camp, he went first to his parents. When they saw him, they shouted with joy for they thought their boy had died. Immediately, they announced there would be a celebration.

21

Before attending the feast in his honor, Little Bear returned to the place where the bear was waiting. As the boy approached, the bear rose. They stood before each other. Gently, the bear touched Little Bear's hands and breathed his spirit into him.

"Now we are brothers," he said
to Little Bear. "Whatever happens
to you will happen to me, and
whatever happens to me will
happen to you." With these words
the boy and the bear parted. They
never saw each other again.

As the years passed, Little Bear became known as Bear Man. Many stories were told about his skills as a hunter and a warrior. He became a great Doctor among the Pawnee because he knew the secrets of healing.

24

Bear Man often held the Bear Ceremony. He performed the Bear Dance to renew his healing powers and to thank the Creator for the bear.

Eventually, Bear Man passed on the powers of the bear to his children and grandchildren so that the ceremony would continue.

26

He lived to be a very old man. On the day Bear Man died, the Pawnee say that not far away, an old bear died, too, in the same way and at the same moment.

Traditional Pawnee Life

The Naming Ceremony

At birth, Pawnee children were given a child's name, and then at adolescence, according to personality and abilities, a new name was given. Throughout their lives, the Pawnee were given many names, which changed according to the deeds they performed or their outstanding achievements.

Hunting

All Pawnee boys were given a bow, arrows, and a shield so that they could learn to protect and feed themselves at an early age. They began hunting small game as soon as they were big enough to hold a bow and shoot an arrow. Later, they learned how to hunt buffalo. When they were old enough, they accompanied the older men on hunting parties. Usually after adolescence, boys began painting their shields. Each shield told the story of the carrier's life. Because the Pawnee were very territorial people, whoever crossed their land or hunted on it was viewed as an enemy.

Bears and Bear Doctors

To the Pawnee, the bear was a symbol of strength and power. It had no equal in the animal world. The

bear possessed great healing powers. Those among the Pawnee who received instructions from the bear to cure illnesses were called *Bear Doctors*. They were revered in the tribe as the most powerful of all Doctors. They were members of the Bear Society.

Bear Doctors conducted ceremonies to renew their healing powers. In the ceremonies, they would paint themselves red or yellow, the colors associated with the bear. The Doctors believed that when the bear breathed in sunshine, it exhaled red and yellow dust.

Around their necks, the Doctors wore bearskins with the bear's head over their right shoulder. In their left hand they carried a *cedar branch*, which they pretended to hide behind as they imitated the movements of a bear in the woods. They also carried a *medicine bag*, which was a piece of hide containing all the objects they needed in healing ceremonies.

Cedar

Cedar is a large evergreen tree. In the Bear Dance, parts of cedar are used to drive disease away, give blessings, and insure long life. Cedar is used in many different Pawnee ceremonies. Its purpose changes according to the ceremony.

Houses

In the past, the Pawnee lived in portable tipis when they were out on a hunt. When they were at permanent camps, they lived in round earth lodges. An earth lodge was made of a wooden frame covered by branches, grass, and earth.

Clothing

According to Pawnee custom, everyday clothing for a woman was a wrap-around skirt with the opening on the right, a sleeveless overblouse, leggings fastened at the knees, and moccasins. On special occasions, a woman wore the daily dress but added elaborate decorations consisting of beads, porcupine quills, ribbons, and other colorful ornamental objects.

The everyday clothing for men consisted of a loin-cloth, leggings, and moccasins. On special occasions, men wore their basic clothing in addition to a number of ceremonial trappings, which signified a special work or achievement.

About the Storyteller

My name is Lynn Moroney. I am a writer and a storyteller, and like many people in my state of Oklahoma, I have Native American ancestors. I am very proud to be a citizen of the Chickasaw Nation. In Oklahoma, there are many Indian Nations. Each nation has its own language, customs, traditions, and stories. And while in these ways Native American people differ, most share an admiration and respect for the bear. In this Pawnee story of long ago, we learn that bears taught many sacred lessons to Little Bear. Even now, bears still teach great lessons to us all.

Lynn Moroney

For many years, Lynn Moroney has captivated audiences with her retelling of star legends and sky myths from around the world. As a seasoned performer, she has appeared on radio, television, and at schools, libraries, and folktale festivals throughout the United States and Mexico. As an educator, she has conducted numerous teacher workshops integrating the study of the arts and sciences. Ms. Moroney is the author of three books: *The Boy Who Loved Bears*, *Baby Rattlesnake*, a retelling of Te Ata's famous Chickasaw teaching tale, and *Elinda Who Danced in the Sky*, an adaptation of the Estonian folktale of the Milky Way. Her fourth book, *Moontellers*, will be published by Northland in the spring of 1995.

About the Artist

From the first time I picked up a pencil, drawing came naturally to me. I am thankful that the ability to paint has given me the opportunity to reach millions of children through this story. Children are, after all, the most important thing in life.

As a member of the Pawnee Tribe, I take great pride in the fact that my paintings are helping preserve a culture that is almost lost. I feel it is important for all children to have an opportunity to learn about their heritage. My father, Henry Chapman, translated the book *The Lost Universe*, which is about Pawnee life and culture. He also provided the translation for several other books about the Pawnee. The symbol I use after my name ⋔, I credit to him. In the 1940s, he found an ancient Pawnee parflesche (a rawhide bag or case) with this symbol on it. The curved line stands for the Vault of the Heavens, and the line in the center represents the Breath of Heaven.

CHARLES W. CHAPMAN ⋔

Charles W. Chapman's thorough research into his Pawnee heritage is evident in the visual beauty and historical accuracy of his oil paintings. Of special interest are his Pawnee Doctor paintings set in the past, which depict Pawnee Bear Doctors conducting their ceremonies. Chapman's paintings have won numerous awards and are part of private collections and galleries across the country. His work was exhibited at the White House in 1989.